Why AM I HERE

MELVIN BELL

ME
WE

MORE EXCELLENT
WAY ENTERPRISES

Scripture references are taken from the King James Version of the Holy
Bible unless otherwise noted.
Pronouns for referring to the Father, Son and Holy Spirit are capitalized
intentionally and the words satan and devil are never capitalized.

Publisher:
MEWE, LLC
Lithonia, GA
www.mewellc.com

First Edition
ISBN: 978-0-9864235-4-3

Library of Congress Number: 2017909203

For Worldwide Distribution
Printed in the USA

DEDICATION

To my Lord, Savior and King, Jesus Christ, who chose me before I was born and called me and ignited His purpose in me. I will never know why He chose me, but I'm so glad He did. He changed my life in the here and now and throughout eternity.

To my lovely wife, best friend, lover, and partner in life, Quinn. You saw potential in me long before I realized it. Your love has truly inspired me to live a life of purpose. You are a gift and I love and cherish you!

To my lovely daughters, Natasha and Cheri. You gave up a lot growing up in our household, and I'm so proud of who you've become. You've made pursuing God's purpose worth it.

To my parents, Hester & Mary Bell. God used you to bring me into this world. Your example of living for God and living a life of purpose has made it easy for me to do the same. I can't thank you enough. I love you.

To my Spiritual Father Millard F. Byrd, for your time every Tuesday pouring into me Godly wisdom. You launched me into my pursuit of purpose and I'm eternally grateful.

CONTENTS

ACKNOWLEDGEMENTS

I would like to thank Elders Troy & Nicole Logan, who have encourage and pushed me to walk in purpose year after year. You have proven to be true friends.

I am thankful to the members of Power of Purpose Christian Center. It has been your support that made me strong in the darkest of times and helped keep me on the journey of transforming purpose. You are the greatest!

FOREWORD

It has been said that the greatest tragedy in life is to be born and not know why.

The title of this book, Why am I here? Practical Steps to Discover Your Purpose, presupposes that the reader is interested in beginning a life- transforming journey toward discovering purpose. Therefore, if you are holding this book in your hands, you should be forewarned that it is not by happenstance. Perhaps it's destiny beckoning you forward or a subtle prodding from within that comes in the form of a whisper from God that says "Follow Me."

What exciting and awe-inspiring possibilities lie ahead!

In *Why Am I Here? Practical Steps to Discover Your Purpose*, Melvin Bell provides unique, thought provoking insights, with interspersing scriptures, that illuminate a lifetime of knowledge he has gained through years of tireless servanthood.

I have personally known Melvin Bell for more than twenty years, and I have found him to be a man of unwavering faith and impeccable character. In an age where there appears to be a general incongruity in our society between what we say we value, and what people actually value, we need men and women of uncompromised character like never before.

Abraham Lincoln once said, "Character is like a tree and reputation like its shadow. The shadow is what we think of it. The tree is the real thing." I can without hesitation say that Melvin Bell stands as an oak in the church world today!

Melvin has written a masterful literary interpretation of what it truly means to begin a journey toward finding purpose. I believe this book will serve as a one-stop resource and spiritual guidebook for all who are truly seeking an answer to the universal question, Why Am I Here?

Why Am I Here? Practical Steps to Discover Your Purpose is a divinely appointed work that will transform all who read it and apply its truths. It is profound because it is a clear and prayerful exposition of understanding Kingdom Purpose.

It is a personal letter from God to each of us individually, for we were all created with a custom mold – a roadmap that does more than give directions, but frames the journey. And it is a journey worth taking.

Troy Logan, Owner
Strike First Fitness

INTRODUCTION

The late Dr. Myles Munroe once said, "If you don't know the purpose of a thing, you will abuse it." After hearing those words and giving them some thought, I wondered just how many people, myself included, were abusing their lives because they had no idea why they were here. For how many people had a lack of purpose, or even the search for meaning, led to destructive behaviors, aimless wandering, and endless frustration? How many times have we endured the rat race of life just to come home at the end of the day and ask ourselves, "Is this all there is?"

As a pastor, many people have asked me over the years how they can find meaning in life, how they can figure out what they were put here to do. My answer has always been that God's "Kingdom Purpose" for our lives is not static, and discovering that purpose is a journey with unexpected twists and turns.

The term Kingdom Purpose comes from Matthew 6:33, where Jesus is teaching his disciples about the burden worrying puts on our shoulders. He told them to instead seek the Kingdom of God.

Now, at first that may seem like a religious platitude, but I promise you, it's not. Our comprehension of purpose really does become clearer over the course of our lives as we grow closer to God. Although God establishes our purpose before we are born (Jeremiah 1:5), discovering that purpose, like life, is a journey. On the way, you discover more about yourself, learn more truths about God, and find the purpose He chose for your life.

Oftentimes, God will lead us on a journey that moves us into areas we never thought about or imagined, which then triggers an awakening of our spiritual passions. For instance, the Hebrew Scriptures tell the story of Nehemiah, who was a Jewish cupbearer to Artaxerxes I, the king of Persia. Nehemiah never expected that anything more remarkable could happen in his life than to serve as cupbearer to a foreign king. It was a high-ranking position in a powerful royal court. He had achieved a great position in life, one that perhaps he thought he'd serve in for the rest of his life. He was happy and had the job of his dreams. God had other plans for him, though—the job as a cupbearer was merely a stepping stone to his true purpose.

Nehemiah learned that the Jews who were left in the kingdom of Judah were experiencing great distress and hardships, and that the walls around Jerusalem, the capital city of Judah, were broken and on fire. This bothered Nehemiah so much that he wept, mourned, fasted, and prayed for days. He then petitioned the king for permission to go back to Jerusalem to rebuild the city. Artaxerxes gave permission for Nehemiah to go rebuild Jerusalem. Nehemiah rebuilt the city in 52 days, despite intense opposition from enemies on all sides.

Although Nehemiah never originally intended or planned to have a hand in rebuilding the wall of Jerusalem, God knew how useful Nehemiah would be and awakened in him a longing for that specific mission. God's Kingdom Purpose for our lives is just like that. We discover His plans and desires as we journey, *actively* pursuing the work He is doing in the world for His people and those He will redeem.

And so, self-examination is important. As you journey, there are questions you need to ask yourself. For over twenty years I have learned about pursuing God's purpose, and I know that if we answer these questions without bias or reservation, God's purpose for each of us will be manifested in the answers in due time.

You will hopefully discover those answers as you work through this book and embark on *the transforming journey of finding purpose!*

Melvin Bell

1

PAUL'S PERSONAL INSIGHT OF THE JOURNEY

Be not thou therefore ashamed of the testimony of our Lord, nor of me His prisoner: but be thou partaker of the afflictions of the gospel according to the power of God; Who hath saved us, and called us with an holy calling, not according to our works, but according to His own purpose and grace, which was given us in Christ Jesus before the world began, but is now made manifest by the appearing of our Saviour Jesus Christ, who hath abolished death, and hath brought life and immortality to light through the gospel. (2 Timothy 1:8–10)

The book of 2 Timothy is a letter written by the apostle Paul to Timothy, a man Paul met on one of his missionary trips. 2 Timothy is probably the last epistle Paul wrote while in prison before the Roman government executed him. Paul knew his death was imminent, but he accepted his end since he would die for the furtherance of the Gospel (2 Timothy 4:6).

Paul was a father figure and mentor to Timothy, who had come to Christ after Paul's visit to Lystra when his mother and grandmother likely converted from Judaism. He took time to share the secrets of God with the young man, teaching him spiritual truths and leadership principles.

As a result of their close relationship, when Paul knew his death warrant had been signed, he wrote to Timothy and used what would no doubt be his last chance to send a message out to his comrades.

More than anything, he wanted to instruct Timothy and remind him of things that would strengthen his faith and enhance his leadership capabilities. Paul understood well how a child of God could carry out the purpose of God in every aspect of life, and he wanted to make sure that Timothy would do just that.

What Paul understood is that discovering God's desire for our lives is not a once-in-a-lifetime event; it is a journey, carried out over time as we face experiences and challenges that God has preordained for our ultimate good. The end goal, our utmost purpose, is to transform into and conform to the image of God's Son, Jesus Christ. This is what God is after.

Paul gave insights about the transforming journey to purpose in his final epistle. At the beginning of the letter, he introduced himself by saying:

> *Paul, an apostle of Jesus Christ by the will of God, according to the promise of life which is in Christ Jesus, to Timothy, my dearly beloved son: Grace, mercy, and peace, from God the Father and Christ Jesus our Lord. I thank God, whom I serve from my forefathers with pure conscience, that without ceasing I have remembrance of thee in my prayers night and day. (2 Timothy 1:1–3)*

As Paul said, he learned something about the transforming journey to finding purpose from his ancestors: the importance of worshipping God with a pure, or clear, conscience.

Clear Conscience

When Paul said that he worshipped God "with a pure conscience," he meant that the way he lived his life did not cause his conscience to nag at him. He felt confident as he sought God's purpose. He knew he was faithful to Christ, to His ministry, and to the pursuit of God. So, Paul boldly declared, "I serve God with a clear conscience." Likewise, as we embark on our journey to finding purpose, our conscience has to be free.

Several years ago, a popular set of Verizon Wireless commercials showed a guy testing signal strength in different locations. He went to places like a swamp, a tall office building, and even a manhole – anywhere that might have poor reception – and he asked the popular question, "Can you hear me now?" For us, we must clear our consciences and seek God's purpose with our whole hearts so that when He calls to us and asks, "Can you hear Me now?", we can know with assurance that we *can* hear Him and are ready to respond to the purpose He reveals to us.

The beginning of success, of finding God's purpose for your life, is knowing God for yourself. When knowing God and living for Him is the starting point for pursuing our purpose, we are beginning the pursuit with the understanding that God holds the key to every worthwhile endeavor, and that He charts the course for every man and woman. We're acknowledging that we need a personal connection with Him to discover who we are and what we were created to be in Him. And an aspect of knowing God is a clear conscience. Whatever clouds your mind or your heart will keep you from seeing the light He sheds on your path.

Paul even affirmed this principle. He was able to fulfill his purpose – but not without declaring that he had a clear conscience. In 2 Timothy 4:7, Paul stated that he had fought the good fight, kept the faith, and was ready to offer up his life as the final sacrifice of his ministry. Knowing he was going to die, he declared that he believed he had fulfilled all that God had called him to do. But … all of that started with establishing a clear conscience before God (despite his horrendous past), and to do so, he had to begin a real relationship with God, and then had to continue living in a way pleasing to Him.

Paul lived and ministered with a clear conscience, but many people aren't able to attain such a thing. Often, when we get off course or altogether stop the journey God has given us, the reason behind our failure is the lack of a clear conscience. We cannot connect with God and serve Him if we cannot hear Him. When God asks, "Can you hear Me now?" what can you say when you have buried your conscience far under your sins or your desire to control your life yourself? If you drown out your conscience, when God asks if you can hear Him the answer is an unequivocal no!

Your effectiveness in the Kingdom of God and your ability to fulfill His purpose hinges upon you having a clear conscience. Are you haunted by past sins? Are you harboring guilt or a grudge in your heart? Or have you bought into lies, such as nurturing an inferiority complex, or allowing yourself to feel that your spiritual life is not up to par and never will be?

If you never commit to clearing your conscience, your legs will remain too weak to walk the full length of the path to finding your purpose.

If anything is hindering you from hearing God clearly, you have already been given the power to change. That is the essence of the Gospel: forgiveness and reconciliation with God. The Gospel is God's empowering tool to us, that if we allow it, helps us take hold of forgiveness and freedom. With repentance and a clear conscience before God, you can listen to the voice of your King and begin (or continue) your journey to the purpose that will totally transform your life.

Sincere Faith

In 2 Timothy 1:4–5, Paul writes, *"Greatly desiring to see thee, being mindful of thy tears, that I may be filled with joy; When I call to remembrance the unfeigned faith that is in thee, which dwelt first in thy grandmother Lois, and thy mother Eunice; and I am persuaded that in thee also."*

Another point Paul made to Timothy was to remind him of the importance of an unfeigned faith, or a sincere faith. To achieve your purpose, above all you must have a sincere faith. Many people who turn to church and religion for help have a problem in the way they view the concept of faith, which leads them off course. They think that faith's chief purpose is to help them get what they need in the moment, like making sure that their bills are fully paid or that they have a good career. But the faith Paul talked about in his letter is much more than something as ordinary and self-interested as our bills or careers. Paul spoke about faith as a lifestyle. What he called faith was not expecting that God would meet our physical needs of the moment (although God can and will do that); rather, he talked about a faith as a means that sustains those who aim to bring glory to God, to do what God has called them to do, and to pursue God's purpose for their lives.

Faith as a means is an *active* faith. It does something. It commits itself to bring glory to God in the pursuit of His purpose. That means that in your work, sincere faith commits yourself to being a person of integrity. With your friends and family, or interacting with anyone in our world, sincere faith commits you to acting with integrity, humility, and love.

Without sincere faith, you cannot grab hold of the purpose God has specifically chosen for you. Without sincere faith, you have no good testimony by which you can say, like Paul, "I fought the good fight, I've kept the faith, and now I'm ready to be offered up." Without sincere faith, you will waste the good that God wants to give to you, and you will cripple yourself instead of finishing the transforming journey of finding purpose.

The Gift of God

In 2 Timothy 1:6, Paul said, *"Wherefore I put thee in remembrance that thou stir up the gift of God, which is in thee by the putting on of my hands."* Everyone has a divine purpose to serve. God has filled you with understanding and certain strengths that allow you to achieve the plans He has for your existence in this world. Even if you only count the blood of His Son, He has still invested so much in you that you will not fail. And that investment is why Paul charged Timothy to not let the grace of God remain dormant, but rather to "rekindle the gift" God had placed in him.

When I was growing up, instead of central heating, my grandparents had a fireplace in their home. To get warm, they would start a fire and gather around the hearth. In those days, while we clustered around the fireplace, my grandfather would tell us stories – and every time the fire started to die, my grandfather would take a poker and prod the fire. As he stoked the dimming embers, the flames would get higher and stronger in intensity, burning bright again.

What Paul told Timothy was not meant for him alone. His message is for every one of us. If we are faithful and stir up what God has already placed within us, it will ignite and blaze, connecting us with God and His direction for our lives.

We should pay attention to Paul's lesson to keep our faith hot and to pay attention to the gift that God has given us, the passion put inside our souls to reach our purpose. Some of us have let the fire go out, and some barely have any burning. Paul knew such things could happen, and that's why he charged Timothy to stay vigilant over the altar of his heart lest the fire go out.

Paul knew there would be challenges in Timothy's life, just like there will be challenges in your life. You, like Timothy, will be tempted to quit or slow down on your journey and you will be tempted to let the fire diminish, but all the same you have got to stir up the fire inside you. Rekindle the gifts you have received from the Lord. God has given you everything you need for the glory of His Kingdom … you just have to keep the fire burning!

Courage

Verse 7 of the first chapter of 2 Timothy says, *"For God hath not given us the spirit of fear; but of power, and of love and of a sound mind."* In the New Revised Standard Version of the Bible, *"sound mind"* is translated as "self-discipline" because having a sound mind means that you not only remain calm but also practice moderation and self-control. It is easy to lose focus and discipline when we go through sufferings and the challenges of life. However, a sound mind helps you to be self-disciplined, to keep to your calling and not wander off course during your journey no matter the challenges you encounter. Your ability to stay focused and keep your fire alight despite obstacles and suffering is important if you ever want to finish well.

In verse 8, Paul further told Timothy, *"Be not thou therefore ashamed of the testimony of our Lord, nor of me His prisoner: but be thou partaker of the afflictions of the gospel according to the power of God."* Paul knew that many people would be dejected or confused by his imprisonment, but he also knew that he was not a normal prisoner – he was a prisoner of Christ. More to the point, he introduced the concept of relying on God in times that seem to the world like failure and ruin – because doing so is one way we partake in the sufferings of Christ, and that takes courage.

No matter how long you've been a follower of Christ, you must understand that sometimes the purpose of God will only come about through suffering. God's transforming purpose for you could be revealed through the fruit of your labor in your present challenges and pain. Paul told his son in the faith that even someone powerfully used by God has to go into discouraging places and still rely on God's plan and goodness. Sometimes, God allows his children to pass through tough times so He can perfect His will in their lives. Never once did Paul suggest to Timothy that his ministry would always be happy, or that he should try to avoid difficulty. Instead, he asked Timothy to join him and embrace the will of the Lord. Likewise, you should cling to God even when the journey leads you into difficulties, because embracing the purpose of God includes walking through many challenges meant to further His everlasting glory and your own reward.

A Salvation of Purpose

In 2 Timothy 1:9, Paul clarifies the intentions of the God he relies on: *"Who hath saved us, and called us with a holy calling, not according to our works, but according to His own purpose and grace, which was given us in Christ Jesus before the world began."* Even in his trial, Paul affirmed that God saved each of us for a definite purpose. We were saved for more than a one-time faith conversion, but many people, including Christians, don't understand this. Because of that lack of understanding, many stumble about in life, unable to find God's purpose for their existence.

Some people feel a calling, that they ought to be doing more and ought to be getting more out of life, but sadly, they never understand the purpose they should strive for. God saved everyone for a purpose, and you must discipline yourself to pursue that purpose. By His grace, He saved us and called us, meaning that He gave us an invitation to join Him in His redeeming work, which we do when we show others the One who reconciles us unto Himself by living our lives to His Glory and pursuit of His purpose. This invitation is a holy calling, and not one to take lightly.

Whether you're a pastor, an elder in your church, a singer, a layperson, or whatever else, you must handle the calling of God, which is pure and righteous, in a holy manner. You must treat it as sacred, not optional. Even if you think of what you are doing as simple or unimportant, it is not. Whether you're participating in a small event in the community or volunteering to clean the bathrooms in your church, whenever you do something in the name of the Lord, remember to carry it out in a pure and holy way.

Humility

Verse 9 has more than simply a description of God: *"[He] saved us, and called us with an holy calling, not according to our works, but according to His own purpose and grace, which was given us in Christ Jesus before the world began."* The verse reminds us that we have not done anything to deserve what God has done for us or what He has called us to do. Everything we receive from Him we receive as a result of His grace.

Oftentimes, people become prideful once they begin to achieve and attain notable accomplishments. When God uses them, when things seem to be "going their way" – maybe they even gain some fame or recognition – they forget that God is the mastermind giving them each success. We should remember, however, that when a success distracts us from our true purpose, it does not come from God and He is not as pleased with our accomplishments as we are.

Whatever you are and whatever you have, each and every faculty you possess, comes from God. As C.S. Lewis wrote in *Mere Christianity*, "[i]f you devoted every moment of your whole life exclusively to His service you could not give Him anything that was not in a sense His own already." He has invested in you so you can make a good impact on those around you and point others to the One who made *them*, not so you can seek out accolades or feel good about yourself. In other words, God's gifts to us are not for our self-interest. Unfortunately, some of us withhold ourselves from doing good…we don't seek to add value to others, spiritually or otherwise. We don't give everything we have for the Kingdom. We keep some things and gifts for ourselves to make our lives more comfortable.

Once you understand that your gifts are not self-given but God-given, you will understand that those gifts are not meant to be self-serving, but instead meant to be Kingdom-serving. Jesus called us according to *His own purpose and grace*. Jesus Christ chose to give us His grace in the beginning before the founding of the world. Before your birth, He determined His transformative purpose for your life. One of the greatest joys of life is that a mighty God has chosen you, and cherishes a gracious, beautifying plan for you. All you need to do is discover it. God is not trying to hide it from you—He waits to guide you forward on this journey, walking beside you so you are never alone and so you, through His strength, are capable of completing all of the tasks He has for you.

Love of God

How God transforms men and women on this journey of purpose is hinted at in Romans 8:28: "*And we know that all things work together for good to them that love God, to them who are the called according to His purpose.*" All things work together for our good because God works in situations and circumstances; He does not merely sit back and watch from afar.

Even when you mess up, there is no need to despair. God still loves you, and in spite of your past mistakes, you should be ready to keep His commandments. He knows your heart, and as the Good Shepherd, will work out everything so that no matter how far you wander from His purpose, He can bring you back.

God is not concerned about *your* ambitions; He's trying to fulfill His own, perfect purpose. Therefore, His efforts will help you rise above your past and work through the consequences of your mistakes so you can think right, behave right, and live right again.

When you resolve to let God work through the good and bad, you can finally accomplish what you need to accomplish. God is able to work through you if you are willing to work with Him. Take Romans 8:28 to heart: all things, the good and the bad, work together for the ultimate good if you love God. Loving God is easy to recognize, too. "*By this we know that we love the children of God, when we love God, and keep His commandments. For this is the love of God, that we keep His commandments: and His commandments are not grievous"* (1 John 5:2–3). If you love God, you should follow His commandments, and through your obedience He will show you the purpose He has for you.

A New Image

As you set off to find God's purpose for you, you must make sure you know what the end result of your life is supposed to be. The Scripture says, *"For whom He did foreknow, He also did predestinate to be conformed to the image of His Son that He might be the firstborn among many brethren"* (Romans 8:29). Sometimes we get caught up in what role we need to take in our church or local fellowship, which often leads to us getting distracted, trapped, and limited by the wrong focus. God has much more in mind than a mere title or membership for you— His purpose is to conform you to the image of His Son.

God loves to bring us closer to the image of Christ. Admittedly, the process is hard. God has chosen a straight and narrow way for His people, but we often decide to go a different route in an attempt to avoid pain, suffering, confusion, and disappointment. So many distractions crop up everywhere and sidetrack us. Our immediate goals often conflict with eternal plans. The change from a complacent lifestyle to a lifestyle of sincere faith can look stressful, uncomfortable, messy, and even dangerous.

Although the process is painful to our flesh, we should not allow ourselves to bypass the straight and narrow path. We are commanded to put off the "old man" – our self-interested focus and desires – and put on the "new man" created in the image of Christ, in righteousness. Merely pretending that you are free from your weaknesses helps no one, least of all you. Few of us have embraced the total freedom of the new man yet, but that doesn't mean that we don't continue to try. *"What shall we say then? Shall we continue in sin, that grace may abound? God forbid. How shall we, that are dead to sin, live any longer therein?"* (Romans 6:1-2).

Go through the process and let God work in you. Let Him remove the anger, resentment, or bitterness from your heart and replace it with forgiveness. Instead of carrying the bondage yourself, you can forgive and be free. Let Him remove lust from your heart, the passion for money, power, things, people, or sexual relations not meant for you, and replace it with wisdom, compassion, and selflessness. Instead of wallowing in desire, you can practice kindness and self-control. Let Him remove jealousy from your heart, the obsession with having pleasures or material things you do not own, and replace it with self-sacrifice.

God possesses the key to radically transform our habits with His grace, replacing all the many things that weigh us down, hold us captive, and turn us off the right course. He can strip every obstructive thing out of your life so you can hear Him when He calls you, and directs you to His Kingdom Purpose for you.

If you attempt to fix your problems yourself, you will eventually run into a dead end. Lust for illicit sexual relations, for instance, cannot simply be solved with marriage. Some people cheat on their spouses or descend into a pornography addiction because they have not given their hearts to the Lord and broken the addiction to the sin they brought into the marriage relationship.

The Lord alone can lead the way around and out of such pitfalls. His Word and His presence are there to break the destructive habits you have formed over the years, if you will let Him.

Despite the difficulty and distress you might face, you have to let go of everything that is not of God.

Some sins or bad habits are much more subtle than others, and you might think of excuses for why they aren't a problem. Idolatry, for instance, might bring to mind bowing to a golden statute, but it exists in many other forms. Your idol could be fashion, TV shows, exotic cars, money, sports, celebrities, or even your friends and family. Whenever we choose to invest our lives in something apart from God, we have made that thing an idol. Even within the Church, we oftentimes magnify things above God, like our traditions and doctrines or our leaders and events. If you have idols, then you can never fulfill your God-given purpose, and His desires will slip further and further away from your heart. Whatever in this world grips your heart, occupies your thoughts, and rules your life is something that stands between you and worshipping the true and living God. If we genuinely desire to fulfill our purpose, we must do away with all idols, and replace them with a total commitment to Christ our King.

Pleasing God requires the dedication of a disciple. Think about the faithful disciples of Jesus – even though they did not always understand, even though at times they wandered off the right path, they gave up their lives to follow Him and, in the end, they did not miss their mark. They stuck to divine purpose, even though that meant they were killed as martyrs for their bold, sincere faith. They had a tall mission: to spread the message of Jesus across the world. They were tasked with starting the church and ensuring that this new, fledgling religion thrived and survived the first century. And to do that, they had to leave behind everything and everyone, including their loved ones. This was a unique mission, and they trusted that God would take care of their families and everything else. They relied wholly on the One who had saved them and summoned them to work alongside Him. If they had idolized anything else, including their self-serving desires to lead comfortable lives, they would not have been wholly committed to God and His purpose. You too need to abandon every reservation that is holding you back, and simply trust that God will take care of everything. Note that although the disciples were a unique case, our commitment to God includes our commitment to take care of our families, particularly spiritually. God's purpose does not cause us to abandon those whom he has entrusted into our care. God will never use your gift to build resentment against Him in others! You cannot use God as an excuse to neglect those around you.

You might not understand what God is trying to achieve through you, but press on. There are many challenges on this road, but none of them should dishearten you. That's why Paul told Timothy to join him in his suffering. God owns the road of purpose – he *created* it, and He will always mold and shape those who choose to walk on it until they are conformed to the image of Christ and receive the hope that is promised to them.

During the experience of conforming us to the image of Christ, you will be shaped and molded into something that fits God's purpose for your life. Sometimes this is painful, but the pain is never without reason. Never decide on the easier way, leading away from Him, even if you are despairing or exhausted. Even if you cannot hear His voice, even if everything looks blurry and gloomy, keep up the good fight to conform to His image, so you can follow Him with a clear conscience. Eventually, as you seek His will, His intentions will become clearer.

God never asks us to do what He is supposed to do. All He expects is our total commitment so He can transform us to fit His purpose. Once the Lord removes the unfruitful parts of your heart, you will be well-prepared to move forward in what He has called you to do. After the transformation by God's grace, you will not be the same person you were before. Your outer appearance may be the same, but your inner person will have a brand new image because you will be filled with heavenly virtues instead of vices and other manifestations of moral decline. You will be filled with forgiveness, kindness, love, and all the attributes that God has refined in you along the way. Removing the things that are not of Kingdom value and replacing them with Kingdom virtues takes time, so your transformation will occur over time, not all at once – this is why discovering your purpose is a journey.

The journey of a lifetime is long, and at times you may feel frustrated and worn out. Just remember, your traveling companion is God, and He is still at work. If you stay connected to Him, you will find refreshment in His presence that will empower you to go on. *"Repent ye therefore, and be converted, that your sins may be blotted out, when the times of refreshing shall come from the presence of the Lord"* (Acts 3:19). You might struggle in some areas of your life, but that is a sign that God is still working on you. All you have to do is make up your mind that you will stay on the right road and follow God's instructions. The importance of sticking to this transforming journey is that God's purpose mirrors Himself, and He is the only way to true fulfillment in this life. With Christ in your heart as your Lord, Savior, and King, you will always have the ability to fulfill what God has called you to accomplish.

2

THE BIRTHPLACE OF PURPOSE

Finding the answer to the question "How do I find the purpose God has for my life?" starts first with understanding that God's purpose always relates to the furtherance of the Kingdom of God. All believers need to understand that their Kingdom Purpose stems from the heart of God, our King.

Isaiah 44:1-2 states, *"Yet now hear, O Jacob My servant; and Israel, whom I have chosen: Thus saith the Lord that made thee, and formed thee from the womb, which will help thee; Fear not, O Jacob, My servant; and thou, Jeshurun, whom I have chosen."* In this text, God speaks to His servant Israel, and, ultimately, to us, this truth: "I have formed you in your mother's womb."

Isaiah 44:24 and Isaiah 49:5 reinforce this, and coupling that fact with how Jesus has redeemed us through grace to live in His purpose, there is no doubt that each of us has been created specifically by God to fulfill the purpose He has chosen for us. We must be prepared to seek the will of the King so that we may please Him.

Jeremiah 1:5 also shows the intimate involvement God has in the life of every person: *"Before I formed thee in the belly I knew thee; and before thou camest forth out of the womb I sanctified thee, and I ordained thee a prophet unto the nations."* Although this verse speaks of Jeremiah's purpose alone, the principle can be applied to every person within God's plans.

We are known to God long before we know ourselves and He has formed us in the womb to be exactly what we are meant to be. God has handpicked each one of us and fashioned us in every way to be able to carry out the purpose He has in mind.

The Scripture makes it clear that God forms His own children to be servants with specific roles in the purpose of His Kingdom.

Unfortunately, at times we want to be something other than a servant in the Kingdom of God, and thus we lose the chance to employ the true value embedded in our core being.

When I was in middle school, I had a friend who was considerably intelligent. While growing up, however, instead of exercising his innate abilities, he did everything he could to fit in with the crowd. He would talk loudly, often disrupting his classes, and he would deliberately not do as well as he could on exams. My friend, in an attempt to blend in with his peers and earn their approval, acted in a way that was contrary to who he really was. Before judging him, however, ask yourself if you are striving to follow the calling of God and become the person He configured you to be, or if you are distancing yourself, even unconsciously, from God's purpose for your life.

From the beginning of time to now, God is trying to tell us all, "I formed you in My image, I have shaped you in the womb, and before even that, I knew you." As a result, your purpose will be found within the heart of God, because He made you and guides you forward with that purpose in mind. You will never find satisfaction with anything less than pursuing, discovering, and fulfilling His plans for you!

Ask the Right Questions

When we ask the wrong questions, we do not get the answers we most need. Founder of IBM Thomas J. Watson has been quoted as putting it this way: "The ability to ask the right question is more than half the battle of finding the answer." Likewise, as you look for your Kingdom Purpose, the best thing you can do is to ask the right questions in the right way. Instead of asking, "What is *MY* purpose?", pose a question that seeks the will of the King instead – ask, "God, what is *YOUR* purpose for my life?"

Or, like the Apostle Paul asked, "Lord, what wilt Thou have me to do?" The difference between the questions might seem negligible, but when the emphasis is put on God, the right answers will become much clearer and more direct.

Oftentimes we get too wrapped up in "SELF," becoming more concerned about what we want for ourselves than about what God wants for the Kingdom. Whenever our will is contrary to His, we are forced to decide if life is more about us or more about the Lord. His purpose is so much bigger than us—and the entire planet, for that matter—and although we are so small in the scheme of things, He wants to manifest His purpose through us on earth. To find the real purpose for our lives, we must learn to put His will first.

Jesus led the way by example in this matter, as in many others. He knew God's purpose by looking first at what God was doing. *"But Jesus answered them, 'My Father worketh hitherto, and I work.' Therefore the Jews sought the more to kill Him, because He not only had broken the sabbath, but said also that God was His Father, making Himself equal with God. Then answered Jesus and said unto them, 'Verily, verily, I say unto you, the Son can do nothing of Himself, but what He seeth the Father do: for what things soever He doeth, these also doeth the Son likewise'"* (John 5:17–19).

Jesus never fell short of or stepped beyond the work the Father intended for Him, because He followed the work the Father did Himself. You can do the same, if you stay connected with God and replicate what He does. When you do that, you will begin to walk in whatever He called you to accomplish.

Another question to help bring clarity to discovering God's purpose in your life is, "God, what are You presently doing in my life?" Too often we are satisfied with coming to a church fellowship, clapping or raising our hands, and hearing a message that suits our opinions. Such things are not enough to bring you closer to your Kingdom Purpose. You must inquire of God, "What is it that *YOU* want in my life?" If you actually look around yourself and search for the movement of God, you will start to find your answers.

Your local fellowship can reveal a sense of God's direction to you, if you ask yourself what He is doing through the Church. Your home, your job, and other places where you spend your time can also present opportunities for how He wants to use you and how He wants you to proceed from where you already are. By understanding what God is doing in different areas around you and how they all interconnect with your calling, you can do as Jesus did and join the Father in carrying out His work in your life. As you begin to work as He works, you will head in the right direction and your Kingdom purpose will be manifested.

Instead of looking at positions like pastor, deacon, or elder as the only way to lead a spiritually fulfilling life, focus on what God is already doing in the life you currently lead and join in His efforts there. Maybe you will eventually end up in a career inside the church, but first meet God where you are. He is always working, everywhere. You can join in that work, like Jesus did. "Whatever He's doing, I do likewise" (John 5:19).

You cannot remain caught up in your own agenda while also desiring God's purpose for your life. As a result of our sinful nature, we are predisposed to want to do things the way we want, whenever we want. We have our own dreams, goals, and interests, and though they may seem harmless, they always get in the way if they are not handed over to God.

In Matthew 26, Jesus set the example for us again. He struggled between what He knew He needed to do and what He wanted in that moment. *"O My Father, if it be possible, let this cup pass from Me: nevertheless not as I will, but as Thou wilt"* (Matthew 26:39). He acknowledged that the situation was not about Him or His desires, but about what God would work through the circumstances, and so He accepted God's will.

One of the most important questions to answer, in all sincerity, is this: are you truly ready to submit to God in any way comparable to what Jesus did? When you look for the purpose God has for you, are you sure you are willing to find His desire and pursue it? Have you been faithful in the pursuit of what God wants and asks of you directly? In order to find the Kingdom Purpose meant for you, you have to learn to be faithful in the small things as well as the large. He reveals His purposes to those who are prepared to receive them. Are you?

You Must Be Faithful

When we talk about wanting our purpose in God, we must face the fact that God wants us to give over everything in our lives to Him. If you want your purpose, you must ask for God's will to be done in every aspect of your life. He wants us to be ready to do His will, and He tests our hearts and readiness all the time. He asks, in subtle or overt ways, "Do you prefer your job over Me? Do you prefer your children over Me? Do you prefer your spouse over Me? Do you prefer your amusements over Me? Do you prefer anything over Me?"

God desires you to be faithful to Him. He wants you to show up, ready to serve. He always rewards faithfulness and draws away from the unfaithful. That could very well be the reason why certain things have not yet been revealed to you: He does not entrust His purpose to the unfaithful. Luke 16:10–11 explains it this way: *"He that is faithful in that which is least is faithful also in much: and he that is unjust in the least is unjust also in much. If therefore ye have not been faithful in the unrighteous mammon, who will commit to your trust the true riches?"* You must be faithful over the small things God has already given you so that He can lead you to the "true riches" of your Kingdom Purpose.

What if the way you use what you have already been entrusted with is preventing you from effectively discovering and pursuing your Kingdom Purpose? Remember, we need to show up and push through even when we don't feel like it because someone else may be depending on us. God may want to use you to help others, but those people you are supposed to help will not receive the help they need if you decide not to show up when they need you. God wants you to be ready to go wherever, whenever, to execute your Kingdom Purpose, even if it means working when you are tired or going out of your way to be of service. When you're tired, think about the bigger picture. Remember that when we push through our feelings, our emotions, and our physical limitations, God will often energize us to finish what He wants us to do!

Our time is a precious resource. We cannot allow distractions like watching television to take up endless hours of our lives. When we get caught up in recreational activities, we miss key windows of time that might have been used to witness to others, attend church, read the Bible, or pray. You know you have spent too much time on entertainment when you know more facts about that than you do about Jesus. When you create time to indulge in leisure activities, but not enough time for God, you have become unfaithful.

Another example of unfaithfulness is how we spend our money. We spend our money on entertainment, fancy clothes, cars, even things we have no business buying at all - the point is that we spend our money on just about anything we want. However, many times when it comes to helping the church or our brethren monetarily, we are reluctant or make excuses. Most churches struggle to get necessary funds to feed the homeless, help the community, and do ministry – remember, as a member of Christ's body and local church, it is our responsibility to support it. We cannot function without each other, and the church cannot function without you and your support.

Now is the time for the faithful to get to work. A single glimpse at current events and the trends in our society is all that is needed for you to realize that God's work needs to flourish here. The simplest and most straightforward method of working alongside Him is to share God's love and show people Jesus. Too often, we are caught up in criticizing people for their faults instead of seeking to show them the redemption we know. God has compassion for every person, and He is waiting for us to practice the same compassion.

Imitating Jesus includes speaking about His grace and love. Pattern your life after Jesus, realizing that doing so may require you to make many adjustments. Living faithfully always requires some changes from what feels most natural to you. If you are volunteering in the community or at church – or in whatever project you find yourself in – examine your heart, and ask yourself whether you are doing it for yourself, to feel good about yourself, or to have others say good things about you – or are you doing it to serve God's people the way He does and to imitate His love to those around you. This is what it means to serve with faithfulness. It's mindfulness. Whether in a church project or off on your own, you never know who God will bring into contact with you so your actions, faith, and love will touch their lives.

God does not reveal Himself or His purpose to those who are not faithful because they do not think about Him or His Kingdom, but only of themselves. Some come to Jesus so they can benefit themselves. They believe God will bless them with manifold blessings of money and other things, but material things are no reason to turn to God. The things of this world are not on equal levels with the things of His Kingdom. You cannot hold onto God and also hold onto what you want in this world. You must surrender your desires and habits to Him, and cultivate a faithful heart.

Connect with the Purpose of God

You must have a connection with God that allows you to see His purpose for your life. In John 15:4–5, Jesus declares, *"Abide in Me, and I in you. As the branch cannot bear fruit of itself, except it abide in the vine; no more can ye, except ye abide in Me. I am the vine, ye are the branches: He that abideth in Me, and I in him, the same bringeth forth much fruit: for without Me ye can do nothing."*

Those who abide in Him—who live through Him, dwell with Him, remain connected to Him—are the ones who can accomplish things of true value. You are the branches and He is the vine.

Branches are fed nutrients through the stem, are kept fast in storms, and are enabled to grow when attached to the vine. The moment they are cut off, they start to wither. They can no longer continue to produce anything. The moment they are no longer connected to the vine, the source of life, even if at first they look no different than before, they have already started to die.

When you desire God's purpose, abiding in the Lord is foundational. You have to stay connected to God always, or else you begin to regress the moment you step away. Some people try to use God as a platform, a stepping stone, a place where they can gather strength before striking off on their own. Some might abandon Him altogether, while others simply say they are busy living life and can't be attached to Him all the time. You cannot allow yourself to enter that mode of thinking—because when you do not abide in the Lord, your spirit starts to wither.

"Take heed, brethren, lest there be in any of you an evil heart of unbelief, in departing from the living God" (Hebrews 3:12). To be faithful to God requires maintaining a connection with God by abiding in Him and following His statutes. Merely knowing about God means nothing if you do not live out His will and desires. King Solomon was a man endowed with unearthly wisdom and insight. He wrote multiple books in the Old Testament, spoke directly with God, and carried out the dream of his father David to build the temple in Jerusalem, as God said he would – but he eventually let life and pleasures distract him, and he drifted away from abiding in the Lord. All of his wisdom amounted to nothing, and his slipping away resulted in a revolt within Israel that tore the country in half.

Jesus not only told us to abide in God, He showed us example after example of what it means to do so and how empowering such a life can be. During His trial in the wilderness, He showed how well He knew the Word and how intent He was to live it out to the fullest. During His ministry, Jesus preached no message other than what magnified His Father. Even during His last few days before He made Himself a sacrifice for all mankind, He prayed with intensity and submitted Himself in obedience to the will of His Father.

You too need to learn how to abide in the will of the Lord and stay connected to Him. *"0 God, Thou art my God; early will I seek Thee: my soul thirsteth for Thee, my flesh longeth for Thee in a dry and thirsty land, where no water is"* (Psalm 63:1). Just as the psalmist said, begin to look for the source of your life and purpose with all-consuming need. Like the branches that rely on the vine to bring them water, look to God for sustenance, guidance, and support to keep growing each day towards the purpose He has for you. Even though some of us do not make consistent time to spend with God, we still hope to do great things for Him and to hear Him clearly. You have to delve into the Word of God, the Bible, and accept every word God says so He can give you the support and strength you can receive only from Him.

For me, the strongest memory I have of the invaluable aid that stems from a connection with God is from a time of grief. My mother-in-law, with whom I had a very close relationship, passed away suddenly. Of course, life goes on, and I had to go to work regardless of my mourning. I arrived in the parking lot of the church office with tears in my eyes, but despite that, I had to push through and work- because I had someone there in need of counsel.

I remember sitting in that office talking to a man. He told me that his mother had just passed, and I struggled to maintain my composure. What he said stirred my emotions, but I still had to minister to him. It had to be the power of God that helped me, because I have no idea how else I did it, but I had to suppress my own grief so I could begin to minister and continue ministering to him. Whether I cried later or not, I knew I had to be present with that man in his grief in that moment. I had to encourage him with the Word of God right then, and by doing so, I could conquer my own weakness through Jesus Christ who loved me. As I listened to the grief of another, I prayed, "Lord, you know what's going on. You have to help me. You have to strengthen me, Lord. I have to convey the Gospel. I have to speak. Help me control my emotions, help me stand firm. I have to speak, Lord. I must be strong."

In my moment of need, God filled me with the strength I needed. He is ready to fill you, too, with all you need, be it strength or compassion or confidence or self-control. You need only to seek Him out and abide in Him continually to have His help and guidance when you need it, to carry out your purpose or to discover what He wants you to do.

God accepts no excuses, none at all, when He calls us to carry out His purpose—but glory be to God, He always supplies us with what we need to carry out His purpose. *"...His divine power hath given unto us all things that pertain unto life and godliness, through the knowledge of Him that hath called us to glory and virtue"* (2 Peter 1:3). When we are faithful and stand till the end, our connection with God, the Giver of purpose, will enable us to achieve and obtain what we must.

Avoid Distractions and Ungodly Behavior

As children of the Most High God, we must acknowledge that there is no great divide between engaging in the ungodly behavior of the world and finding enjoyment in watching it from the sidelines. Instead, remember to fill your minds with *"whatsoever things are true, whatsoever things are honest, whatsoever things are just, whatsoever things are pure, whatsoever things are lovely, whatsoever things are of good report; [and] if there be any virtue, and if there be any praise, think on these things"* (Philippians 4:8).   Sometimes even our hobbies can become obsessions, and God can (and is often) forgotten as result. Just because something you do or watch is "clean" does not mean it is beneficial to you.

Your connection with God must always come first. That doesn't mean, for example, spending five minutes on devotions before sitting down for an hour-long show. Where you spend your time indicates where your heart is and what it treasures. Becoming overly concerned with anything other than God leads to a disconnect from the One who gives purpose to everything.

Prayer and study of the Word of God will reveal your purpose. When you pay attention to Him, He rewards you by feeding your soul.

God successfully works in and through you when you are connected to Him. He wants to work in you so you can succeed in your Kingdom Purpose. Whenever your conscience suggests that you have let something come between you and God, God is trying to tell you to surrender that something to Him. You need to be ready to get rid of whatever holds you back and weakens your connection to the Lord.

You can know you are close to God if you are ready to shout and praise Him despite the troubles in the world and in your own life—that shows clearly that you have stayed glued to God, because you are deriving your joy from Him and not from the other things. You are not the same person you were in the past; don't go back to being that person again. If you stay faithful in your connection to God, He will fulfill His purpose through you.

3

PURPOSE AND YOUR RELATIONSHIP WITH GOD

"Be not thou therefore ashamed of the testimony of our Lord, nor of me His prisoner: but be thou partaker of the afflictions of the gospel according to the power of God; who hath saved us, and called us with an holy calling, not according to our works, but according to His own purpose and grace, which was given us in Christ Jesus before the world began, but is now made manifest by the appearing of our Saviour Jesus Christ, who hath abolished death, and hath brought life and immortality to light through the gospel" (2 Timothy 1:8–10).

God places an enormous amount of value in our relationship with Him. He has gone through everything necessary to make a relationship with us possible: *"who hath saved us, and called us with an holy calling, not according to our works, but according to His own purpose and grace, which was given us in Christ Jesus before the world began."*

Our purpose is found through a relationship of love with God. You must love God to discover your Kingdom Purpose. Because He has already laid the foundation for this relationship, you only have to respond to Him as He reaches out to you. Love is the greatest virtue, as recorded in 1 Corinthians 13:13: *"And now abideth faith, hope, charity, these three; but the greatest of these is charity."* The word "charity" here does not mean the giving of money, but rather the unstinting, wholehearted affection and love between people and God. This kind of love would be impossible for us to achieve if God had not extended it to us already: *"We love Him, because He first loved us"* (1 John 4:19).

The well-known verse John 3:16 states, *"For God so loved the world that He gave His only begotten Son, that whosoever believeth in Him should not perish, but have everlasting life."* Because most people are so used to this verse, they tend to forget the powerful truth it contains. God giving up His only Son for the sake of those who did not care then, for many who would never care afterward, and for those who would never fully appreciate what He had done, is staggering. It means that He cared more about providing the gift of eternal life than about what He had to give up to accomplish our redemption. He reached out to us long before we could reach back, because He loves us.

The first epistle of John describes the same selfless act of God, but expounds on it further: *"Beloved, let us love one another: for love is of God; and every one that loveth is born of God, and knoweth God. He that loveth not knoweth not God; for God is love. In this was manifested the love of God toward us, because that God sent His only begotten Son into the world, that we might live through Him"* (1 John 4:7-9). The apostle told us that love is the foremost attribute a Christian can show, and that without it, we do not know God at all. The proof we have that love is so important to God, so fundamental to who He is, is the sacrifice of Jesus for our sins so that we can live instead of perish. That is the truest love, and that is what we are called to emulate by surrendering our lives to Him.

We can understand how to love Him best when we remember that it was not we who first loved God, but He who loved us and sent His Son to atone for our sins. By that love we are called to love: *"Beloved, if God so loved us, we ought also to love one another"* *(1 John 4:11).* Even though we cannot see God now with our physical eyes, if we love one another, we can see the power of God at work in us.

Do not trick yourself into believing that you can love God while you don't love the people around you. Again, the apostle John sheds light on this subject: *"If a man say, 'I love God,' and hateth his brother, he is a liar: for he that loveth not his brother whom he hath seen, how can he love God whom he hath not seen? And this commandment have we from Him, that he who loveth God love his brother also"* (1 John 4:20-21). You cannot love God when you harbor hatred, resentment, or animosity toward others. We shouldn't be concerned about their status, personality, background, upbringing, or anything else. Regardless of who they are, you have to love them. In order to love God, you must love your brother also.

When love exists between you and God, you can carry out your journey of transforming purpose with confidence. John 5:20 says, *"For the Father loveth the Son, and sheweth Him all things that Himself doeth: and He will shew Him greater works than these, that ye may marvel."* In other words, the love of God is established first, and then comes the revelation of what God is doing. Because God loves His Son and is loved in return, He shows His Son the purpose He has. Likewise, when you have a real relationship with God, an active love, then God will show you things that you would not otherwise have a chance to see and be a part of.

The Father is always working. He is always on the move. The reason we often miss that is because we don't have the eyes to see that which we ought to see, or the ears to hear the voice of the Holy Spirit trying to communicate to us. Our lives become so cluttered with mundane worries, objects, and distractions that we cannot see the things of the Kingdom. When our love for God is strong, then we can see and hear what He wants to share with us.

Essentially, the relationship we have with God is like a two-way street. God loves us, and because He loves us, we love Him. Once you start to love Him in earnest, you can begin to know what God has in store for you. If you disdain your relationship and only want things from Him, or if you do not give proper attention to building the relationship, God will not reveal His purpose for you.

A loving relationship with God leads to more than just affection, and Jesus presents the perfect example to follow to have an effective relationship with God. He displays three essential characteristics we need to mirror: obedience, communion, and devotion.

Obedience

Because of the relationship of love Jesus shared with the Father, Jesus committed Himself to obedience. *"But that the world may know that I love the Father; and as the Father gave Me commandment, even so I do" (John 14:3).* He knew that the surest proof of that love was to obey, and He expects the same of us: *"If ye love Me, keep My commandments"* (John 14:15). Without obedience, love cannot exist in you – and without love, you cannot see God's Kingdom Purpose for your life.

Jesus came to the world for one purpose, and one purpose only. *"Wherefore when He cometh into the world, He saith, 'Sacrifice and offering Thou wouldest not, but a body hast Thou prepared Me: In burnt offerings and sacrifices for sin Thou hast had no pleasure. Then said I, Lo, I come (in the volume of the book it is written of Me,) to do Thy will, O God'" (Hebrews 10:5–7).* He came to do the will of God, and when we are conformed to His image, we also commit ourselves to doing the will of God. We cannot simply do things that look spiritual—we have to follow the calling of God and keep His commandments.

In the book of Samuel, King Saul learned very well that God is not fooled by spiritual posturing as opposed to actual obedience. God told him to destroy a city for its wickedness. However, Saul did not carry out the full will of God, but bent God's instructions as he saw fit.

"But Saul and the people spared Agag, and the best of the sheep, and of the oxen, and of the fatlings, and the lambs, and all that was good, and would not utterly destroy them: but every thing that was vile and refuse, that they destroyed utterly" (1 Samuel 15:9). Saul and his followers did the easy thing—destroying what they did not like but keeping what was useful to them. More than that, Saul offered an excuse when Samuel demanded why the livestock remained: *"They have brought them from the Amalekites: for the people spared the best of the sheep and of the oxen, to sacrifice unto the Lord thy God; and the rest we have utterly destroyed"* (1 Samuel 15:15).

Saul suggested what sounded like a great idea, a spiritual idea, but that did not transform his disobedience into righteousness. A good idea is nothing but trouble if it doesn't have anything to do with God. Sometimes, we think up wonderful ideas—but if they are not within God's will, if they are in opposition to what He wants from us, those ideas are wrong and dangerous.

Saul completed only a portion of what God had commanded him, and hoped that would be good enough. *"And Samuel came to Saul: and Saul said unto him, 'Blessed be thou of the Lord: I have performed the commandment of the Lord'"* (1 Samuel 15:13). What he did not realize was that performing only half of the commandment was no different than performing none of it.

"And Samuel said, 'Hath the Lord as great delight in burnt offerings and sacrifices, as in obeying the voice of the Lord? Behold, to obey is better than sacrifice, and to hearken than the fat of rams. For rebellion is as the sin of witchcraft, and stubbornness is as iniquity and idolatry. Because thou hast rejected the word of the Lord, He hath also rejected thee from being king'" (1 Samuel 15:22–23).

Saul lost his kingdom on earth because of his disobedience. How much worse for us, who know of the damage of disobedience, if we lose our share in the work of God's Kingdom.

When God instructs us, sometimes we do not have directions as exact as what Saul received, but God makes sure we can understand Him, if we are ready to listen. Still, many of His instructions are as obvious as the ones He gave Saul – the Scripture is filled with such instructions that reveal the will of God.

What do you do, then, when there is no exact verse to help you make a decision? Jesus explained to His disciples how they could continue to grow in their relationship with God and follow His leading even after He was no longer with them in person:

I have yet many things to say unto you, but ye cannot bear them now. Howbeit when He, the Spirit of truth, is come, He will guide you into all truth: for He shall not speak of Himself; but whatsoever He shall hear, that shall He speak: and He will shew you things to come. He shall glorify Me: for He shall receive of Mine, and shall shew it unto you. All things that the Father hath are Mine: therefore said I, that He shall take of Mine, and shall shew it unto you (John 16:12–15).

When you have received Jesus Christ as your Lord and Savior, you too have the Holy Spirit to guide you. By the Spirit, you are shown what God desires for you and how He expects you to act.

Because our true purpose does not belong to us, but rather to God, the Holy Spirit shows us where we need to go and what we need to do. The Spirit provides our moral compass, then acts as a guide to help us find out what more we can do for God with our lives. If you do not obey God in the obvious things, how can He show you the less obvious? Therefore, obedience is crucial as we develop our relationship with God and seek His purpose for us. *"Seeing ye have purified your souls in obeying the truth through the Spirit unto unfeigned love of the brethren, see that ye love one another with a pure heart fervently: Being born again, not of corruptible seed, but of incorruptible, by the word of God, which liveth and abideth forever"* (1 Peter 1:22–23).

Communion

Obedience comes only when you understand what God has decreed, and to do so, you must spend time communing with God. Striving to become closer to God leads us to His purpose for our lives.

Jesus, during His trial in the wilderness, had to face temptations from satan that were meant to trick Him into disobedience. Jesus not only had close fellowship with God when they were together in Heaven, but He maintained that fellowship with His Father all through His earthly life (such as when the boy Jesus had stayed behind in the temple at Jerusalem to "be about His Father's business" as told in Luke 2). Because of this, Jesus knew how to handle the deception and temptation meant to destroy His sinless nature.

As He fended off satan's attack in Matthew 4, He referenced a verse from Deuteronomy that has great implications for us: *"That He might make thee know that man doth not live by bread only, but by every word that proceedeth out of the mouth of the Lord doth man live"* (Deuteronomy 8:3b). The way to truly live is by heeding the Word of the Lord and following Him in everything.

"Communion" does not always mean partaking of the bread and wine—sometimes it is used to reference intimacy. Paul spoke of a holy communion in 2 Corinthians 13:14. *"The grace of the Lord Jesus Christ, and the love of God, and the communion of the Holy Ghost, be with you all. Amen."* He desired the followers of Christ to experience not only the grace of Jesus and the love of God, but the communion of the Holy Spirit.

The word used to express "communion" in that verse was the Greek word *"koinonia,"* which means "participation, fellowship, and sharing." The verse says that what happens when the Holy Spirit interacts with believers is a mutual sharing between you and God.

"Communere" is the same word the Bible uses for a husband and wife coming together intimately. That is also a method of communing with one another, in a committed relationship. That is why the Bible says, *"But whoso committeth adultery with a woman lacketh understanding: he that doeth it destroyeth his own soul"* (Proverbs 6:32). God considers intercourse a very sacred thing, meant only for a husband and wife, because it represents another aspect of the metaphor of marriage, which God designed to give humans a way to understand His closeness

to the Church. Although humans only have such a physical intimacy on earth, the pleasure and goodness of that mutual sharing between spouses helps us to understand the spiritual closeness and bonding that can be achieved through a loving relationship with God.

Communion, even in its broadest sense, is not possible when only one party is involved: it requires mutual participation. God responds when you try to commune with Him and build a relationship. Abraham, who walked with God and followed His directions, serves as an example: God not only acknowledged him, but communed with him. *"And the Lord said, 'Shall I hide from Abraham that thing which I do; seeing that Abraham shall surely become a great and mighty nation, and all the nations of the earth shall be blessed in him? For I know him, that he will command his children and his household after him, and they shall keep the way of the Lord, to do justice and judgment; that the Lord may bring upon Abraham that which He hath spoken of him'"* (Genesis 18:17–19). God does not simply listen to those who seek Him, but responds to them and interacts with them.

Once you establish a close relationship with God, the communion you have with Him will help you along in your journey. As Jesus showed us, when we love God and spend our time with Him, He shows us what He is doing around us and how He wants us to take part in that. Communion helps you know the heart of God. At times, God will grant you understanding of things you would not have known before or never would have thought to ask—and sometimes that will lead you closer to your Kingdom Purpose.

Devotion

The whole time Jesus lived as a Man, He displayed His dedication to the Father. The Father's will came before everything for Jesus, as it should for us. Devoting yourself to someone requires loyalty, and loyalty to God means nothing else can take His place as supreme in your life. In Exodus 20, God declared the Ten Commandments, and the very first was, *"Thou shalt have no other gods before Me"* (Exodus 20:3). He went on to explain in verse 5, *"Thou shalt not bow down thyself to them, nor serve them: for I the Lord thy God am a jealous God."*

If you want to know God's purpose for you, you have to devote yourself to His service, not to the service of other things, people, or even your own self. Straddling the fence or having a lackadaisical attitude about your relationship with God is unacceptable. You have to devote yourself completely. Jesus said in Matthew 12:30, *"He that is not with Me is against Me; and he that gathereth not with Me scattereth abroad."*

You cannot serve God and fulfill your Kingdom Purpose when you are not fully devoted to Him. He asks for everything, but most people try to find a way around that.

We want to know what we can do for God without giving Him everything we have. We want God on our own terms, for God to be committed to us, but we want be free to make our own choices and to be committed to Him only when it suits our feelings.

A frequent problem that arises when you try to figure out God's purpose for you without total dedication to His will is that you look for things you can *do*, instead of looking for who you are meant to *be*.

When you distract yourself with questions like, "Am I supposed to be preaching, or doing something else?" you miss the fact that God's first concern is with the state of your heart and your relationship with Him. God is more concerned about *your being than your doing.*

Jesus chided the Pharisees on many points, but the most memorable is when He called them out for being hypocrites. *"Woe unto you, scribes and Pharisees, hypocrites! for ye are like unto whited sepulchres, which indeed appear beautiful outward, but are within full of dead men's bones, and of all uncleanness"* (Matthew 23:27). Although the Pharisees did all sorts of things that they counted as spiritual, God knew that their hearts were far from Him. They had no devotion to His will, but rather sought their own way.

For example, honesty is a character trait required by God. You can't go to church and pray then go to your place of employment and cheat your employer out of his/her time (by being late, taking longer breaks than you should, etc). Integrity – and the qualities of Christ – should be reflected in *who you are* in every situation in which you find yourself.

You cannot attempt to make your own path to the Kingdom. There are no traditions or rituals that will balance out your lack of devotion. There are no compromises so you can enjoy life on your terms but be just spiritual enough not to run into any problems. God does not give an audience to hypocrites or the lukewarm. You have to commit yourself to the Lord and let nothing stand between you and Him.

With love, obedience, communion, and devotion, you can walk through your life with a right relationship with God and the assurance that you will carry out your Kingdom Purpose. No matter what lies ahead in your path, whatever difficulties or surprises, you can trust in God and believe He will lead you where you need to go.

Purpose Requires You to be Tested

Since God will not use someone whose character is weak, selfish, or hypocritical, your character is an important factor in finding your purpose. Like the Pharisees, many people act holy around their fellow believers, but when they are away from those who would hold them accountable, they act contrary to the Word of God. Due to the double standards of Christians today, folks outside of the Church see no reason to turn to Christ.

Please understand that you are not expected to live a perfect life—but the character you show when no one is looking speaks volumes about what lies in your heart. You need to assess your heart and ask yourself honestly where you stand in the sight of God. Before He will reveal your purpose, He must first prove your character.

The Bible abounds with stories that show many people's successes and failures in holding their moral ground when no one could see them. One of the most well-known stories is the life of Joseph. God had an incredible purpose in mind for Joseph, but before it came to pass, Joseph underwent many difficulties and betrayals that showed what sort of man he was.

At first, he seemed to have everything in life he could have wanted: he was the pride of his parents and had their affection, he lived a comfortable life, and God had given him the gift of prophetic dreams. Then his circumstances changed drastically when his brothers, in a fit of jealousy, sold him into slavery. How would you have dealt with such an extreme betrayal? You're living a fantastic life, and your family sells you into slavery? Life had been great for Joseph, but it quickly turned on its head.

Slavery was not the end for Joseph, however. Because he remained faithful to God and maintained his character while enduring such dire circumstances, Joseph made a good impression on the master of the household, Potiphar. *"And his master saw that the Lord was with him, and that the Lord made all that he did to prosper in his hand"* (Genesis 39:3.) However, even *that* changed. Potiphar's wife tried to seduce Joseph into committing adultery with her, promising him that no one would find out. But, Joseph refused because it was a sin against his master and a sin against God (Genesis 39:9). Potiphar's wife, upset by this, falsely accused Joseph of raping her, and Joseph was thrown into jail!

Even while in jail because of the lies of Potiphar's wife, Joseph maintained his character and God helped him.

> *But the Lord was with Joseph, and shewed him mercy, and gave him favour in the sight of the keeper of the prison. And the keeper of the prison committed to Joseph's hand all the prisoners that were in the prison; and whatsoever they did there, he was the doer of it. The keeper of the prison looked not to an thing that was under his hand; because the Lord was with him, and that which he did, the Lord made it to prosper* (Genesis 39:21-23).

Joseph was in prison for years, but one day Pharaoh, the king, had a dream, and no one could interpret the dream. A man who had served time in prison with Joseph now worked for Pharaoh and remembered that Joseph could interpret dreams. He told Pharaoh about Joseph, and so Pharaoh summoned Joseph to appear before him. Joseph interpreted Pharaoh's dream as meaning that Egypt would have seven years of abundance followed by seven years of famine, and advised Pharaoh to stockpile all surplus grain. The king was so impressed and so grateful that he made Joseph second in command in Egypt. During the famine, even people from neighboring countries came to Egypt for food, including Joseph's brothers. Had it not been for Joseph's dream and advice, many people would have starved, including his family.

Joseph did not know why his brothers sold him into slavery, or why he had to go to prison, but he did not let that damage his character. Even when no one would know the difference, he still did what was right – and only after that did God use him mightily to save innumerable lives. In the midst of Joseph's life trials, God continued to work alongside him and helped prepare him for his purpose, something far greater than what he could have achieved back home as his father's favorite son.

We have chances every day to maintain our character before God. Once, someone blessed me with a check for $100. Although that is not much money, at that time I had a serious financial need. After I cashed the check at the bank's drive-through window, I received the money in an envelope and, because I was in a rush, I did not count the money before pulling away. I decided to verify the amount before leaving the parking lot and realized the teller had made a mistake: She had given me $1,000 instead of $100! I could have tried to convince myself that the money was meant to come to me in my distress, but I knew the Lord did not operate like that. It was my duty to return the extra money. I did, much to the joy and relief of the teller, who would have otherwise lost her job. After I passed that test of character, God gave me many revelations about my purpose. I had proven faithful in my character, so He entrusted me with more.

How you behave under pressure is one of the clearest ways to understand your own heart and your readiness to be used by God. While you may not like the tests, you have to persevere. Some people say they are ready for God to use them, but as soon as pressure comes, they collapse and prove they do not have the character to carry out God's will. You have to exercise self-control over your own reactions before God can use you.

I remember an incident when a young white man called me a "boy." Since I was raised in the Jim Crow South, that name can get under my skin even now. The young man was about the same age as my daughter, and he dared call me a boy. I thank God I didn't choke him (Believe me, I wanted to) or respond hastily and nastily. But, God gave me the grace I needed to show grace to him instead. God had already changed my heart because of redemption, so I was able to face that pressure and triumph. Redemption is the first step towards good character, but tests and trials are what purify us. *"Wherein ye greatly rejoice, though now for a season, if need be, ye are in heaviness through manifold temptations: That the trial of your faith, being much more precious than of gold that perisheth, though it be tried with fire, might be found unto praise and honour and glory at the appearing of Jesus Christ"* (1 Peter 1:6-7).

Be Conformed to the Image of Christ

Our character shows our readiness for God to use us, which is why we must conform ourselves to the image of Christ. *"For whom He did foreknow, He also did predestinate to be conformed to the image of His Son, that He might be the firstborn among many brethren"* (Romans 8:29). God has chosen us to be conformed to the likeness of His Son. That is His first and greatest purpose for us. If you learn nothing more about your

Kingdom Purpose from this book, understand this: *Being conformed to the image of God's Son is the first purpose God has for you.* Start there and build on that foundation, and everything else will follow.

Pressure and trials come because you are meant to conform to the image of Jesus. The tests remove the filth and weight from you, or they show you what your weaknesses are so you can get rid of them. You should not feel depressed by your trials—they are the process God has chosen to transform you into the image of His Son.

Discipleship starts to bear fruit when we make the decision to display moral character in spite of our circumstances. After you make the decision to follow Christ, you begin to learn how to live like Him no matter what goes on in your life. You will find your purpose in God as you move from that starting point to your final destination in the Kingdom.

Problems occur when we try to travel the easy road instead of the path God has ordained-a path of trials and tests you need to face as you conform to Christ. If you try to avoid those trials, you will not receive the empowerment of God that would have helped you through, and later on, because of that shortcut, you will not be equipped with the valuable character and ability God intended for you.

4

THE
CALLING OF
GOD

True purpose is always birthed in the heart of God; only He knows the full course our lives will take and the plan He desires to achieve in every individual. *"There are many devices in a man's heart; nevertheless the counsel of the Lord, that shall stand"* (Proverbs 19:21).

When most people search for their purpose, they cannot find it because they try to discover it apart from God. *"Man's goings are of the Lord; how can a man then understand his own way?" (Proverbs 20:24).* All purpose stems from the heart of God, who has designed each and every person for the life allotted to them. That is why the Lord told Jeremiah, *"Before I formed thee in the belly I knew thee; and before thou camest forth out of the womb I sanctified thee."* Paul had a similar calling from God, as the Lord told Ananias: *"But the Lord said unto him, 'Go thy way: for he is a chosen vessel unto Me, to bear My name before the Gentiles, and kings, and the children of Israel: for I will shew him how great things he must suffer for My name's sake'"* (Acts 9:15–16).

Although Jesus interrupted Paul's life in a magnificent, unique way on the road to Damascus, Paul knew very well that he was not the only one with a specific calling from God. Look again at what he told Timothy:

> *Be not thou therefore ashamed of the testimony of our Lord, nor of me His prisoner: but be thou partaker of the afflictions of the gospel according to the power of God; who hath saved us, and called us with an holy calling, not according to our works, but according to His own purpose and grace, which was given us in Christ Jesus before the world began, but is now*

*made manifest by the appearing of our Saviour
Jesus Christ, who hath abolished death, and
hath brought life and immortality to light
through the gospel* (2 Timothy 1:8–10).

The calling of God, a "holy calling," is extended to everyone who accepts the salvation given by Jesus Christ. There is a Kingdom Purpose for every member of the body of Christ.

Members of the Body

*But all these worketh that one and the selfsame
Spirit, dividing to every man severally as He
will. For as the body is one, and hath many
members, and all the members of that one body,
being many, are one body: so also is Christ. For
by one Spirit are we all baptized into one body,
whether we be Jews or Gentiles, whether we be
bond or free; and have been all made to drink
into one Spirit* (1 Corinthians 12:11–13).

When we come to Christ, we are not made into robots who say and do the same thing. God works with each of us as individuals, which is why we are given the "selfsame Spirit" who works with each person separately. Every believer is unique, but still a member of a single body. Everyone is given different functions to suit their distinctive Kingdom Purpose, regardless of race, denomination, age, intelligence, or anything else. Both black and white are coequal in the Kingdom, as there is no nationality that is above or below another. Jesus looks only at whether the heart is submitted to Him, not at what sort of heritage a person has. Consequently, no racism should exist in the Church; we are all children of the Light, different parts of the same body.

The Apostle Paul used the metaphor of believers being a *body* more than once in his letters, because it is extremely important to take to heart the unity of the Church and the diversity of gifts and callings within it. He stated that we are diverse components of a whole: *"For the body is not one member, but many"* (1 Corinthians 12:14). Though every part of the body serves a different function, all the parts are interconnected and dependent on each other to survive. Paul told us that the body can only operate as a whole, not by focusing on a single, although important, part: *"If the whole body were an eye, where were the hearing? If the whole were hearing, where were the smelling? But now hath God set the members every one of them in the body, as it hath pleased Him. And if they were all one member, where were the body? But now are they many members, yet but one body"* (1 Corinthians 12:17-20).

No matter how great you think your purpose is, it is never independent: it will complement the functions of other believers around you. You might try to pursue your Kingdom Purpose without connection or association with the members of the body, but you will not succeed if you do—the Kingdom is not just for you, but rather for all the subjects of the King. Just as a chopped-off finger or toe cannot accomplish anything, neither would you be able to do much outside of the body. You will lose your vitality and the worth of your actions if you attempt to be a loner while you carry out your purpose.

On the other hand, you might think your purpose is not truly useful. You may look at those in public ministry and wonder why you aren't able to do that too. You forget that the body is comprised of all types of individuals, and many of them work out of the public eye and in humble ways. *"If the foot shall say, 'Because I am not the hand, I am not of the body'; is it therefore not of the body? And if the ear shall say, 'Because I am not the eye, I am not of the body'; is it therefore not of the body?"* (1 Corinthians 12:15–16). Not everyone can be the same thing, and not everyone should be the same thing. Do not strive to perform a certain job you admire: strive to know what function God has set aside for you and has enabled you to do better than anyone else around you for the success of the body as a whole.

When you become part of the body, God bestows abilities upon you so you can carry out your Kingdom Purpose. Everyone has his own share of gifts for his own tasks, and there are many different functions you can fill. *"And God hath set some in the church, first apostles, secondarily prophets, thirdly teachers, after that miracles, then gifts of healings, helps, governments, diversities of tongues. Are all apostles? are all prophets? are all teachers? are all workers of miracles? have all the gifts of healing? do all speak with tongues? do all interpret?"* (1 Corinthians 12:28–30). You should not look for the most exciting or praiseworthy jobs, but rather for what God has already chosen for you.

Remember that just because a role is not prestigious does not mean it is not honorable. The less prestigious roles are often the most indispensable, and receive greater respect from the Lord.

> *And the eye cannot say unto the hand, 'I have no need of thee': nor again the head to the feet, 'I have no need of you.' Nay, much more those members of the body, which seem to be more feeble, are necessary: And those members of the body, which we think to be less honourable, upon these we bestow more abundant honour; and our uncomely parts have more abundant comeliness.*

For our comely parts have no need: but God hath tempered the body together, having given more abundant honour to that part which lacked. That there should be no schism in the body; but that the members should have the same care one for another" (1 Corinthians 12:21–25).

From the world's viewpoint, your purpose might seem lesser or greater than the purpose of others, but that is not true. Your purpose might be considered less "honorable" by the world's standards, yet it is an important component to God and the Church. The body of Christ cannot function to the fullest capacity, as God has intended, without you. Likewise, you need the body's support and aid. All of us are indispensable in the pursuit of God's calling.

Functioning Together

Since we are fashioned to work interdependently within the body, we have to guard against comparing ourselves with each other. Looking at the jobs given to your brothers and sisters can breed discontent and envy because you may want a job other than your own, or, even worse, you may begin to think more of yourself and your job because it has greater rewards or more attention than others.

Whether you have been following Christ for a long time or are new to all of this, you are not above giving to or receiving from your fellow believers. Every member of the body has a function and purpose, and is gifted to be able to carry out that purpose so that, as a whole, the body can perform all its necessary tasks.

For I say, through the grace given unto me, to every man that is among you, not to think of himself more highly than he ought to think; but to think soberly, according as God hath dealt to every man the measure of faith. For as we have many members in one body, and all members have not the same office: so we, being many, are one body in Christ, and every one members one of another. Having then gifts differing according to the grace that is given to us, whether prophecy, let us prophesy according to the proportion of faith; or ministry, let us wait on our ministering: or he that teacheth, on teaching; or he that exhorteth, on exhortation: he that giveth, let him do it with simplicity; he that ruleth, with diligence; he that sheweth mercy, with cheerfulness (Romans 12:3-8).

Paul charged us to not be high-minded, because our tasks and our abilities are given through the grace of God, not because of our own accomplishments or aptitude. He cautioned the Church against falling into pride or self-importance. God works in us, and through that empowerment we can succeed, not by our own merit. We cannot think better of ourselves than of those around us, since God made each of us for our tasks and expects us to work in unity with fellow believers. Your duty is to find your rightful place and lean into that to serve Him and humanity alongside the rest of the body.

When we try to fulfill the purpose of God apart from Him or apart from our brothers and sisters in Christ, specifically those in our local fellowship where we belong, we fail. We do not get to decide how our purpose should be fulfilled any more than we can decide what our purpose is. If we try to isolate ourselves from those with whom we're joined together in a divine covenant, we will not find God's purpose. He did not design us to act that way. Each member derives meaning and purpose from the body as a whole.

Some years ago, I struggled to understand a few things that were happening in my life. Although I was already a pastor of a church, I was still looking for answers as to what certain aspects of my life meant. One Sunday, a member approached me in conversation and pointed out what my gifts were. The person had insight and spoke something valuable to me that I could not have seen on my own, which helped me see things I had always taken for granted. That is often how we discover different facets of our Kingdom Purpose: members of the body support, admonish, pray for, teach each other, and share with each other through what God has given them.

This is why we need to stay together. We are to function as a single body, though we consist of individual parts. For a body to accomplish anything, all its members must work together. The hands only work if the arms support them; the legs only work if the feet will carry them; the mouth only works if the larynx supplies it with voice. Likewise, if one of your legs no longer supported you, your entire body would be forced to limp along, or possibly even crawl.

Take football, for example. When I was in high school, I played offensive guard. In one game in particular, our coach called for us to run a "trap play" to the left, which is a play where every player goes down one person to the right and blocks the player next to them. This leaves the defensive tackle free. Once the quarterback hands the ball to the running back, the running back starts running toward the defensive tackle – who is free because no one has blocked him so far. I was supposed to run across and block the tackle, which would open up a space for the running back to go through and score. But this particular time, when the center snapped the ball, he didn't do it fast enough, and I tripped over his foot, and fell. So essentially, everyone went down, the tackle was free, but no one was there to block the tackle, because I tripped over the center's foot, and the running back got creamed. The center not moving fast enough and me tripping over the center's foot caused the entire team to suffer. Our mistakes, our failure to do what we were supposed to do, affected the entire team. So, as members of the body of Christ, never lose sight of the fact that what you do affects those around you. Your actions or inaction affect the rest of the body.

"That there should be no schism in the body; but that the members should have the same care one for another. And whether one member suffer, all the members suffer with it; or one member be honoured, all the members rejoice with it" (1 Corinthians 12:25–26). As a unified body, the family of God, we have to care for one another. Whatever you do in the Church should promote and nurture your brothers and sisters in Christ. Through this unity, everyone can begin to pursue their Kingdom Purpose in earnest.

Serving with Gifts

God has given us the grace to carry out, through His divine enablement, a specific task or position of responsibility that He has ordained for each of us from the beginning of the world. *"Now there are diversities of gifts, but the same Spirit. And there are differences of administrations, but the same Lord. And there are diversities of operations, but it is the same God which worketh all in all. But the manifestation of the Spirit is given to every man to profit withal"* (1 Corinthians 12:4-7). The gifts, abilities, and opportunities given to us are from God. Don't become caught up in looking for something other than what you have, because the Lord knows everything you can accomplish, and He has chosen a very particular and personalized purpose for you. The Holy Spirit gives to every man what he needs as well as the chance to help everyone around him benefit from what he has – so you need to start making use of that gift!

If you preach, just preach God's message and nothing else. If you help, just help and don't take over. If you teach, just teach and don't control. If you give encouragement, just encourage and don't become bossy. If you are put in charge of something, don't manipulate anyone or mastermind the circumstances. If you are a giver, aid people in distress and be quick to respond.

Don't let yourself become irritated or depressed as you serve, even if you are at a disadvantage. Jesus experienced the same sort of difficulties as He ministered on earth. *"Seeing then that we have a great high priest, that is passed into the heavens, Jesus the Son of God, let us hold fast our profession. For we have not an high priest which cannot be touched with the feeling of our infirmities; but was in all points tempted like as we are, yet without sin. Let us therefore come boldly unto the throne of grace, that we may obtain mercy, and find grace to help in time of need"* (Hebrews 4:14-16). Do not let yourself forget that you have a great honor to serve God through hard and exhausting times. *"And they departed from the presence of the council, rejoicing that they were counted worthy to suffer shame for His name"* (Acts 5:41). Even if you are put to shame or at risk of martyrdom, you can keep a smile on your face by remembering that God has chosen you to work alongside Him, and He will support you in your time of need because He understands your struggles.

If you are unsure of what gifts God has given you for serving Him, take the time to discover what they are. Sometimes, you might find that your calling is in an activity you do not think you're cut out for or called to do. When you do not know what to do, sometimes the only thing you can do is to start working wherever you can. God might eventually reveal to you, "Yes, this was your calling all along." However you begin – whether because of a passion for the work, or a nudge toward it - you will discover what is and is not your calling only after you have started working. What might not have appealed to you in the beginning might be your area of calling after all.

I went through the same confusion before I found my calling. I did not want to pastor a church or stand behind a pulpit and preach. I wanted to do something else, the way I wanted to do it, instead of getting involved in full-time ministry: I wanted to be a businessman and leave pastoring to someone else. I thought I wouldn't be able to handle the burdens associated with pastoral work, like counseling and visitation. The financial services industry in which I worked suited me; I preferred donating to help keep the church running.

The gifts I had, however, were pastoral; I was actually, unconsciously, pastoring people even before I became an official pastor. Already, I had ministered to people in a way that I did not know reflected the heart of a pastor. It was just who I was.

Eventually, I stopped fighting the call and decided to walk into the very thing I hadn't wanted to do at the time. I was cleaning the church one day, and decided to play around in the pulpit. When I stepped into the pulpit, I had an experience with God. It's hard to explain … I felt like I had been there before. I almost jumped back because the feeling was so strong. At that point, a certain boldness and confidence came over me. I knew that confidence was from God, and it didn't matter if I was mocked or what anyone else thought. I'd walked into my purpose from God, and I was sure of it. That day, God confirmed that I was not meant for anything else. I'd wanted to make money in business - preachers did not make much money in those days-but God would not let me move in that direction.

Similarly, your gifts could call you in a direction you never wanted to go, but you will never meet with real victory in serving God until you are following His intentions for you. *"But now hath God set the members every one of them in the body, as it hath pleased Him"* (1 Corinthians 12:18). God decides, not you—and once you stop struggling to find your desired path, you can find the one He has selected for you.

If, along the way, you realize you possess certain gifts that others seem to have, you cannot just decide that your calling matches theirs. You cannot follow the plan laid out for someone else, because God works with individuals separately. He does not simply group people into categories and use them interchangeably. Two people could be called into pastoral work, but they may not have the same ministry: their operations and gifts might be different, according to how God administers them. You cannot compare your gifts to someone else's and know through that what God intends for you. You must instead start working and continue to search for God's specific will for you.

This is why it's important for you to be involved in a local fellowship as you search for and fulfill your purpose. You can serve among other believers, learn from them, and learn about your own gifts. In a properly functioning body of believers, you will have a leader to equip you, brothers and sisters to help you, and teachers to instruct you, and you can in turn serve them. As you serve together with other believers, you will move forward with added support and strength through your journey, and will see more clearly how you can fulfill your Kingdom Purpose.

5

EIGHT QUESTIONS FOR DISCOVERING YOUR KINGDOM PURPOSE

Wondering why you are here on earth is normal. As you seek your God-given purpose, you are putting that instinctual question to its best use-but if you find yourself saying, "I wish God would just show me my purpose," you have fallen into the misconception that God is trying to hide it from you!

Like we learned from Jeremiah and the Psalms, God knew us before we were even in the womb—and He has had a divine purpose for us since then. Jeremiah came into the world with a purpose already fashioned for him and the circumstances of his future: *"Before I formed thee in the belly I knew thee; and before thou camest forth out of the womb I sanctified thee, and I ordained thee a prophet unto the nations"* (Jeremiah 1:5). Because God does not show partiality, He does not pick or choose a selected group of people to work with and through: just like He had a plan for Jeremiah, He has a plan for everyone who comes to Him. Before we were born, God chose a purpose for you and for me! At no point in your life can you stray too far from His calling to find your purpose—there are no limitations regarding what He has already foreseen and incorporated into His designs for you, and the ever-evolving stages of your life could lead you closer to your Kingdom Purpose, if you will let Him guide you. He can always take you exactly where He wants you to be, even if there are twists and turns you never saw coming.

The eight questions below are meant to confirm what He has already put inside you. They serve as a starting point and have helped many people on their transforming journey to reach their Kingdom Purpose. After you read through this section, hopefully you too will find yourself on the right track to discovering your God-given purpose. Make sure to answer the questions honestly and prayerfully so that nothing misleads you.

Question 1: "God, why did You create me?"

First of all, when we try to figure out why we are here, we must start by asking the One who put us here. In order for us to discover our purpose, we must go to the source of everything that exists: God, the Creator of all. *"For by Him were all things created, that are in heaven, and that are in earth, visible and invisible, whether they be thrones, or dominions, or principalities, or powers: all things were created by Him, and for Him: And He is before all things, and by Him all things consist"* (Colossians 1:16–17). Only He can tell you the purpose you were created for, like He revealed to Jeremiah and countless others. Because you need to understand the purpose that guided His decisions on how to form you in the womb and when to put you here, the question you need to ask first is, "God, why did You create me?" You may think that is a simplistic question, but knowing the answer is foundational to your progress. The Scriptures teach us that our only way to reach God and please Him is through Jesus Christ: *"Jesus saith unto him, 'I am the way, the truth, and the life: no man cometh unto the Father, but by Me'"* (John 14:6). The most crucial step in answering the calling of God is to accept His Son as your Lord and Savior. I challenge you to open the Gospels, and read the words of Jesus. I promise that you will be blown away by His wisdom, and enriched by challenging yourself to follow His example. As you learn to follow Christ and His ways, your life will become purposeful, meaningful, and fulfilling. Even without understanding your specific Kingdom Purpose, you can faithfully observe the will of God when you follow Jesus: *"For we are His workmanship, created in Christ Jesus unto good works, which God hath before ordained that we should walk in them"* (Ephesians 2:10).

Because Christ fills your life and your work with meaning, learning your purpose apart from Him is an impossible task. Jesus eloquently described the necessary communion in John 15:5. *"I am the vine, ye are the branches: he that abideth in Me, and I in him, the same bringeth forth much fruit: for without Me ye can do nothing."* Your connection with the Lord—how much you maintain your relationship with Him and pursue His will in your life—is the determining factor in whether or not you can do what He wants you to do. If you have had a poor relationship with Jesus up to this point, you are not deprived of a purpose, nor are you incapable of achieving God's plan even now. The Apostle Paul is an excellent example of this. When he was a young man, known as Saul, he hunted Christians and brought them to the Jewish authorities for punishment and execution. His cruelty to the early Church did not hinder God's plan, however: Jesus interrupted Saul on his way to Damascus, and in an instant, Saul's life was transformed. After a short period of blindness and fasting, Saul met Ananias, who helped him discover one of the first facets of his purpose- to preach the Gospel of Jesus Christ. Later, in a letter to the Galatian church he helped plant, Saul, now Paul after his encounter with God, explained his transformation: *"But when it pleased God, who separated me from my mother's womb, and called me by His grace, to reveal his Son in me, that I might preach Him among the heathen"* (Galatians 1:15-16).

You have a specific purpose, and when you understand why God created you exactly as you are and placed you exactly where you are, then you can begin to understand your reason for being alive. The first part of everyone's purpose is to come to God through Jesus Christ and learn to walk in His ways. When we do so, we can truly communicate with God, and we are primed and ready to discover all the details of His plans for us.

Question 2: "What do I truly have a passion for?"

Merriam-Webster's dictionary defines passion as "an intense, driving, or overmastering feeling or conviction, or an emotion that is deeply stirring or ungovernable." Passion is your key to unlocking your purpose. Passion is not a casual feeling; it's a feeling that compels you, almost forces you, to act on a deeply held desire that you just can't seem to shake off.

Such a feeling is apt to get stronger as time goes by, and it will enable you to endure incredible things when you can find a positive outlet for it. If you seek God and ask Him to give you a way to utilize your passion, you can proceed on your journey by leaps and bounds. As long as your passion matches the calling of God, the intensity of feeling will help you move in the right direction for as long as required. Jeremiah experienced the same sort of internal drive.

God had revealed to him that he was fashioned from birth to be a prophet to many nations, and even when things became hard and people ridiculed Jeremiah for his message, causing his willpower to falter, the passion still remained and encouraged him to continue: *"Then I said, 'I will not make mention of Him, nor speak any more in His name.' But His word was in mine heart as a burning fire shut up in my bones, and I was weary with forbearing, and I could not stay [silent]'"* (Jeremiah 20:9).

The passion of God's purpose burned within Jeremiah and kept him from throwing up his hands and walking away from his calling! Now ask yourself what you have a passion for, what could help you pursue the furtherance of God's Kingdom. What is burning inside of you that you can do for God? That could be God's purpose for you, waiting for an outlet!

Question 3: "What angers me?"

After you spend time in serious thought, prayer, and meditation to discover your true passion, you can take the concept a step further and ask yourself, "What angers me?"

You might doubt that anger could have anything to do with your purpose, but anger can function much like passion. When you find yourself consistently angered by a specific wrong or oversight, you can find the energy and determination to enact a solution.

Keep in mind that anger can be misdirected, and if there is no moral, uplifting way to utilize your anger, then it's probably not a righteous anger that God is moving in you. Anger can lead to many mistakes, so you must be very careful to ensure you direct your anger properly, in a godly fashion.

Moses, who was a Hebrew by birth but had been adopted by the daughter of the Egyptian king (Pharaoh), had been born with the purpose of freeing the children of Israel from slavery in Egypt. His heart was already sensitive to the captivity of his people, so when he saw an Egyptian beating a Hebrew slave, Moses allowed his anger at the wrongdoing to cause him to murder the Egyptian. *"And it came to pass in those days, when Moses was grown, that he went out unto his brethren, and looked on their burdens: and he spied an Egyptian smiting an Hebrew, one of his brethren. And he looked this way and that way, and when he saw that there was no man, he slew the Egyptian, and hid him in the sand"* (Exodus 2:11-12). In the heat of the moment, Moses let his anger overpower him and cause him to sin-but that same anger later helped him stand firm as he struggled against the Pharaoh of Egypt and did his part to deliver the Israelites from slavery, as God intended.

Ask yourself if there is anything that angers you and encourages you to fight against the wrongdoings or injustices around you. Do you feel an anger that aligns with God's will? Is there a way to use that anger to bring about good changes? Because anger is hard to control, be very careful and cautious as you answer these questions. Spend time in prayer as you consider them. Ask God what He would want you to do with your anger – whether to encourage it or to quiet it – and observe how God works in that area of your life.

Question 4: "What breaks my heart?"

As you can see, the emotional response to what happens around you can play a large part in guiding you towards your Kingdom Purpose. When you feel or sense something in more than a casual way, when you want to act and can't ignore what's driving you, then you have a clue as to what you were designed to do.

And part of that emotional response is this question: "What breaks my heart?" You may see or hear things that affect you in a deep and lasting way, whether you understand the reason or not. Something might scream inside your heart, or hang about you like a cloud for days after you learn about it. Whatever the case, anything that moves your spirit to help or correct a situation can act as the catalyst to set you on the right path.

Nehemiah's purpose unfolded in just such a way. *"... Hanani, one of my brethren, came, he and certain men of Judah; and I asked them concerning the Jews that had escaped, which were left of the captivity, and concerning Jerusalem. And they said unto me, 'The remnant that are left of the captivity there in the province are in great affliction and reproach: the wall of Jerusalem also is broken down, and the gates thereof are burned with fire.' And it came to pass, when I heard these words, that I sat down and wept, and mourned certain days, and fasted, and prayed before the God of heaven"* (Nehemiah 1:2–4).

Don't miss that: Nehemiah was simply curious about his homeland when he inquired about the Jews and Jerusalem, but the news he heard affected him to his core. Something awakened inside him and caused him to mourn. His heart was broken by the desolation of his people, so much so that he wanted to act. He started with kneeling before the Lord and pleading for Him to send help to his countrymen in Jerusalem - and not long after, Nehemiah realized he would be that help.

You can recognize the pattern: God often stirs our hearts with strong emotion so we feel compelled to act, and to meet the needs of others. Nehemiah had no original intention to rebuild the wall or even go to Jerusalem. Even when he heard of the need, he thought someone else would do the work. God had other plans in mind, and inspired Nehemiah with strong sorrow so he would be ready to act when the time came. What about you? What breaks your heart? What need do you see that moves you deeply?

Question 5: "What gives me deep inner joy?"

A Dwight L. Moody quote expresses the next principle in discovering your purpose very well: "Happiness is caused by things which happen around me, and circumstances will mar it, but joy flows right on through trouble; joy flows on through the dark; joy flows in the night as well as in the day; joy flows all through persecution and opposition; it flows right along, for it is an unceasing fountain bubbling up in the heart; a secret spring which the world can't see and doesn't know anything about; but the Lord gives His people perpetual joy when they walk in obedience to Him."

You need to look for what gives you joy regardless of your surroundings or circumstances. Positive, reaffirming emotion can give you direction, so your next question is, "What gives me deep inner joy?"

For Paul, life never seemed to let him "catch a break," but he didn't allow the endless challenges to steal the joy he found in fulfilling God's purpose for him. From the start of his ministry to the end, he encouraged people to keep their joy in serving God and fulfilling His purpose for their lives.

When the Lord showed Paul that entering Jerusalem would result in his imprisonment and other difficulties, his friends tried to convince him not to go. Instead of giving in to fear, Paul responded with assurance: *"And now, behold, I go bound in the spirit unto Jerusalem, not knowing the things that shall befall me there: Save that the Holy Ghost witnesseth in every city, saying that bonds and afflictions abide me. But none of these things move me, neither count I my life dear unto myself, so that I might finish my course with joy, and the ministry, which I have received of the Lord Jesus, to testify the gospel of the grace of God"* (Acts 20:22–24). Although Paul knew he would face persecution and imprisonment, he still considered it a joy to finish what God had given him to do.

Is there anything that gives you deep, consistent joy regardless of your situation? It could be a hint towards God's purpose for you. Don't overlook your positive emotions, because we are all given the chance to experience contentment and affirmation in our ministry for the Kingdom, not only struggles and weightiness. Take time to pray about whatever gives you inner joy despite external circumstances—because that could be your purpose!

Question 6: "What gives me a deep sense of peace and accomplishment?"

Everyone enjoys accomplishing something, and no one likes failing. We like to see the results of our work, and sometimes if we cannot see the results immediately, we feel discouraged.

When you are carrying out your God-given purpose, however, you do not always see immediate results. Because of this, you need to ask yourself, "What gives me a deep sense of peace despite the circumstances, and a sense of accomplishment despite the viewable outcome?" If your peace is not contingent upon your situation, if you are not disturbed by working hard at something without obvious developments, then you might have found your calling.

Once, a young married man felt compelled by God to move to another city several hundred miles away so he could open a business there. The decision was difficult to make, because his family and his wife's family all lived where the couple currently resided, and they were all very close. However, after much prayer and discussion between the couple, they moved where they felt led. The man opened a financial services company, which struggled for the first five years—the most financially difficult years that the young couple had ever experienced. The man was tempted to quit and move back home, but in the midst of those challenges, he felt a deep peace that he was where God wanted him to be. He stuck with it, and by the seventh year the business became so prosperous that the man was able to pay off all his debts. In the end, he became a millionaire and helped support many missionaries across the world.

Experiencing peace as you abide in the will of the Lord does not come without challenges and confrontation from the enemy and from others. You can recognize the peace of God because it remains steadfast even when you face opposition, and your conscience encourages you to persevere, even if you don't see the results you expected. Be able to discern your motives – are you trying to satisfy God or please yourself? Discerning your motives will help you recognize and embrace God's peace as you persevere. Continue to move in the direction where you feel peace, and thank God for supplying you with that reassurance. This will allow God's peace to rule in your heart and help move you forward towards your Kingdom Purpose. Prayerfully consider what gives you inner peace and a sense of accomplishment, then allow God to work through you to carry out His purpose for you in His own way.

Question 7: "What theme keeps occurring over and over in my life?"

You do not need a specific talent or hobby to point you in the right direction; sometimes, through consistent reminders, God brings to light certain inclinations you have that He intends to use. Ask yourself, "What keeps coming up for me, over and over again? What has been a recurring theme in my life?"

Several years ago, my mother informed me that my third grade teacher had once told her that she knew I would either be a salesman or a preacher when I grew up. Apparently, every day on the playground, I wound up in the center of a crowd of children, where I talked and kept everyone's rapt attention. I showed leadership potential even back then, and my teacher saw the obvious application: I would either be a salesman or minister.

As predicted from so early on, after I graduated from college with a degree in Business Administration, I owned and operated several businesses. Often when I finished giving a sales talk or holding an opportunity meeting, I would receive the compliment that I "really preached tonight." I didn't want that reminder, because I wanted to focus on business, but other people made similar statements as well. It just kept coming back as a common theme in my life. In the end, my third grade teacher was right on both counts: I have been in sales, and now I'm a minister!

Another example of a recurring theme throughout someone's life is the Apostle Paul, formerly Saul. Like I've mentioned previously, Saul had a passion for Christians – for killing them and persecuting them. He actually thought he was serving God by destroying Christians! Then he had a conversion on the road to Damascus, where God changed his name from Saul to Paul. The same passion Paul had for killing Christians before his conversion, he now used for building the Church! Paul always had an intense passion for God – it was just now funneled in the right direction.

If you look back through your own life, you will be able to see where God has been working in you, speaking to you, and directing you. Maybe you did not have the chance to recognize it before you began truly looking for it, but the harder you look, the more clearly you can spot the recurring themes of your life.

Talk to your relatives about what they remember most about you. Ask childhood or high school friends and teachers what they remember about your abilities, passions, and talents. Look for recurring themes, or anything that comes back again and again throughout your life. God will help you to see what you need to see because He is not trying to keep His purpose a secret from you. Just pray for His guidance and you will find the meaning behind the recurring themes of your life.

Question 8: "Who has God placed in my life to inspire me to follow His calling?"

Some people say, "I don't need anyone but God," but that sentiment is not wholly true. God designed His people to operate in unity, to support each other and the endeavors of the Church. You are meant to contribute to the lives of others, and they are meant to contribute to yours.

People come in and out of our lives all the time, but some people will arrive to help you along in your purpose. Surrounding yourself with people who also follow God's will is important. When you are planted in a local congregation, when you are consistently engaged in a fellowship of believers, you will be in the best place to ask yourself, "Who has God placed in my life to inspire me or prod me in the direction that will lead to my discovery of God's will for me?"

Because of all the imperfect people in churches, you might be tempted to forgo attending altogether—but don't do that! Even though too many people aren't living up to a godly standard, sincere men and women who passionately pursue God and His purpose for their lives still attend, and they are in need of true fellowship with other God-fearing individuals. You cannot use the bad sheep as an excuse to not be a part of some fellowship in your area. In the end, God will judge those who are not sincere, but He still expects us to do our part in the body. He designed us to function with others to complete the purposes of His Kingdom, so we need others to help us discover and fulfill our purposes.

Here's how the Message Bible phrased it:

> *"In this way we are like the various parts of a*
> *human body. Each part gets its meaning from*

*the body as a whole, not the other way around.
The body we're talking about is Christ's body of
chosen people. Each of us finds our meaning and
function as a part of His body. But as a chopped-
off finger or cut-off toe we wouldn't amount to
much, would we? So since we find ourselves
fashioned into all these excellently formed and
marvelously functioning parts in Christ's body,
let's just go ahead and be what we were made to
be, without enviously or pridefully comparing
ourselves with each other, or trying to be
something we aren't"* (Romans 12:4–6).

Each member of the body derives meaning from the others,
which is why our place within the body of Christ is so important.
When you work closely with other people, your purpose and
ministry are made known to them, and they can help you
understand your purpose more clearly. Sometimes others will see
you operating in your purpose long before you do, and they can
help you to find your calling or to leave one not meant for you.
Not every job will suit your gifts, and you are not left without
purpose if the first areas you engage in do not fit your abilities or
calling. Paul addressed this in full in 1 Corinthians 12, which is
worthwhile to read again.

We are all one body, comprised of many members and purposes.
Each person is just as important as another, and God has placed
each and every one in the body with a specific purpose as it has
pleased Him! If you want to find your own purpose, why don't
you plant yourself firmly in a local church, congregation, or other
body of believers in Jesus Christ, and involve yourself in the
ministry available there. Being part of a local fellowship of
believers can be integral in helping you discover your purpose

because, just like one part of your body gives meaning and affects the use of another part of your body, those believers can help you identify your purpose by the way you function among them.

If you commit yourself to the principles you have learned in this book and do not allow yourself to give up, you will surely draw near to our Lord on the road to fulfilling His Kingdom Purpose for you.

However, if you receive nothing else from this book, I want you to remember this: do not torture yourself trying to find your purpose – or that *one* thing that you feel God has created you to do. Instead, concentrate on being like Christ every day in every situation you find yourself in. Live to glorify God wherever you are – at home, at work, in your relationships – and in pursuing Christ's ways in your life and the lives of those around you, God's purpose will find you.

"Wherefore we receiving a kingdom which cannot be moved, let us have grace, whereby we may serve God acceptably with reverence and godly fear: For our God is a consuming fire" (Hebrews 12:28–29).

ABOUT THE AUTHOR

Melvin L. Bell is an advocate, teacher, innovator, and life & leadership coach. However, the title that best describes him is servant leader. True servant leadership is not easy and often unseen, but Melvin has learned over the years that its effect is far reaching and long-lasting.

A devoted husband and father of two beautiful girls, Melvin has spent the last 20 years coaching leaders in the nonprofit sector and mentoring young men. He has traveled across the country speaking on topics of leadership, purpose, and personal development. He speaks with passion, which allows him to connect with his audience and move them to action. His coaching skills are in great demand because he makes himself fully available and asks the insightful questions which lead his clients to advance to the next level in their personal lives, professions, and businesses.

Serving as the lead pastor of a church, Melvin also focuses on meeting the needs of the community and helping individuals fulfill their purpose in life. He is an advocate for those who are economically disadvantaged and has coached groups on relationship-building for over 20 years.

Melvin holds a Bachelor of Business Administration degree, a Master of Theology degree, and an Honorary Doctorate of Divinity degree. He has served as the Senior Vice President and top sales agent at Primerica Financial Services, one of the largest insurance and investment firms in the country. He is also a member of John Maxwell Team. Melvin believes transforming the lives of individuals is essential when aiming to transform our society.

Melvin Bell
Email: melvinlbell1@gmail.com
Linkedin: Melvin Bell
Twitter: drmelvinlbell
Facebook: Melvin Bell